Anne Frank and Her Diary

Biography of Famous People

Children's Biography Books

BABY PROFESSOR

EDUCATION KIDS

Speedy Publishing LLC

40 E. Main St. #1156

Newark, DE 19711

www.speedypublishing.com

Copyright 2017

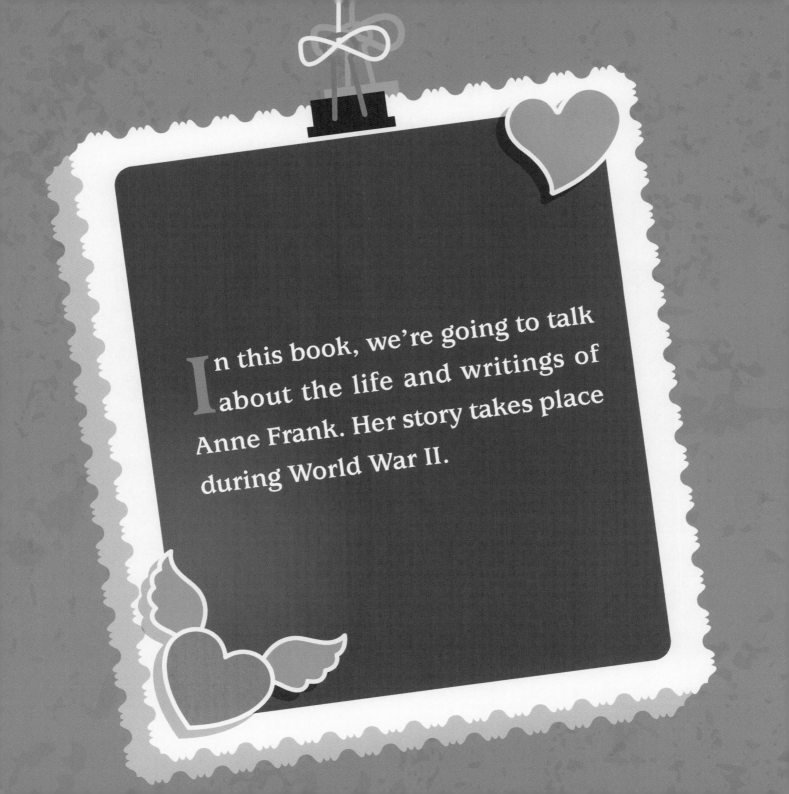

In this book, we're going to talk about the life and writings of Anne Frank. Her story takes place during World War II.

WHO WAS ANNE FRANK?

Anne Frank and her family went into hiding during World War II because they were Jewish. While they were hiding, Anne began to document her experiences in a journal. Later, after Anne had passed away, her father had her journal published and it became famous around the world.

ANNE FRANK

FRANKFURT, 1920'S

ANNE'S EARLY LIFE

Anne Frank was born in the month of June in 1929 and her given name was Annelies Marie Frank. Anne's family was a typical German family in many respects. They lived a happy, calm life in the suburbs of Frankfurt and their neighborhood was made up of people of different religions.

n the past, the fact that her family was Jewish wouldn't have been an issue, but there were changes happening in Germany and soon Anne and her family would be in danger.

JEWISH FAMILY, 1938

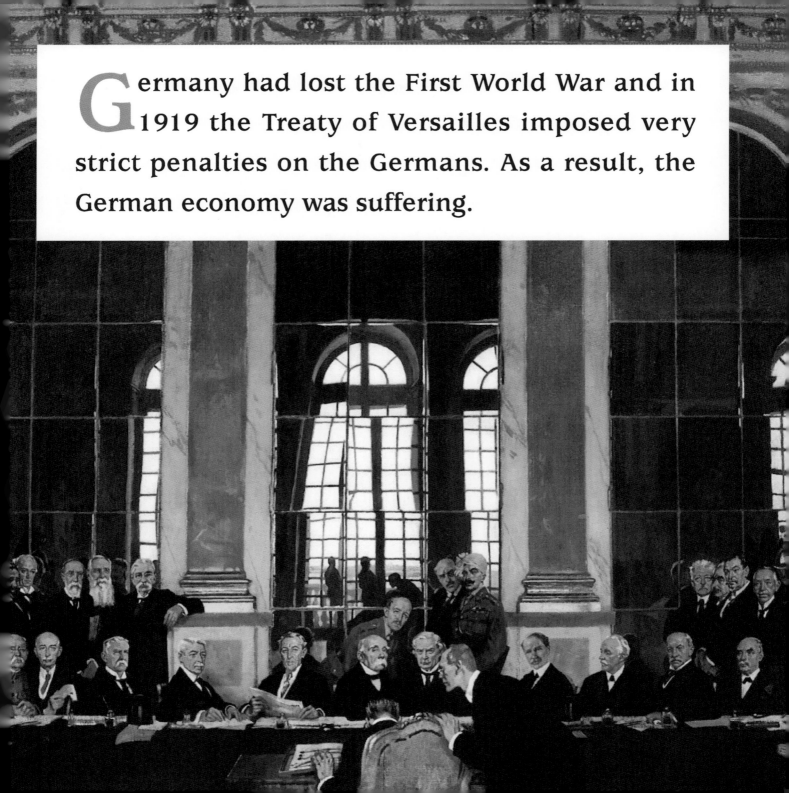

Germany had lost the First World War and in 1919 the Treaty of Versailles imposed very strict penalties on the Germans. As a result, the German economy was suffering.

At this time, a young German who hated Jews was coming into power. His name was Adolf Hitler. He felt strongly that the Jewish people had caused the defeat of the Germans in World War I. He wanted to see them eliminated and a master race of Germans with "pure blood" to form the country of Germany.

NAZI PARTY RALLY GROUNDS (1934)

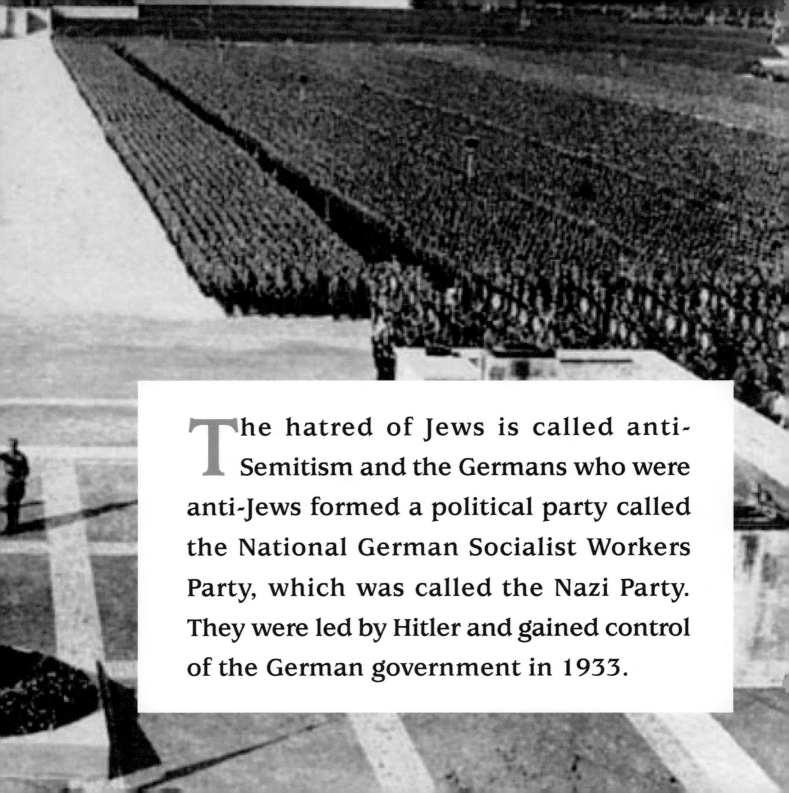

The hatred of Jews is called anti-Semitism and the Germans who were anti-Jews formed a political party called the National German Socialist Workers Party, which was called the Nazi Party. They were led by Hitler and gained control of the German government in 1933.

OTTO FRANK (1968)

nne's father, Otto Frank, later remembered
that in 1932 he had heard groups of soldiers
singing about Jewish blood being splattered.

As soon as Hitler became Germany's chancellor in 1933, Otto knew that he had to move his family somewhere else. He and his family didn't want to leave, but they had to because it would have been dangerous for them to stay.

During the autumn season of 1933, Otto moved his family to the city of Amsterdam in the Netherlands. There, he became the head of a company called Dutch Opekta, which produced products that were used to create jams.

THE BEND IN THE HERENGRACHT
IN AMSTERDAM

ANNE FRANK 1940

After many years of suffering under the anti-Semitic government in Germany, the Frank family once again enjoyed freedom in their new home. Sadly, it was not to last. Anne attended a Montessori School and was very popular. She had Dutch as well as German friends and her friends came from both Christian and Jewish backgrounds. She was very smart and enjoyed learning new things.

WORLD WAR II

On the first of September in 1939, Hitler's troops marched through Poland. This was the first action in a war that would become the Second World War. In the spring of 1940, the Nazis marched into the Netherlands and Anne's new homeland was defeated after just a few days of fighting. Once the Nazis had control of the Netherlands, things began to change rapidly for Anne and her family.

**THE NAZI-GERMAN FORCES
IN THE NETHERLANDS**

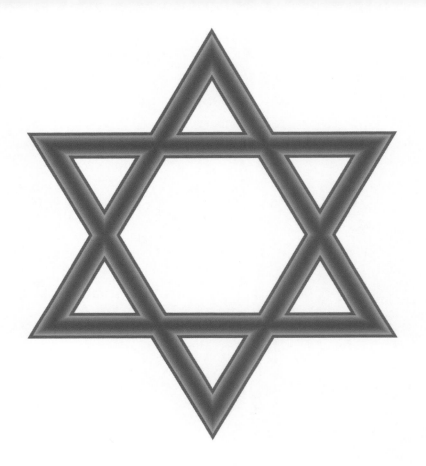

Starting in October of 1940, Jews were forced to wear a Star of David to identify them. This yellow star was supposed to be worn all the time. They were forced to abide by a strict nightly curfew. Also, they were not allowed to own or manage businesses.

Anne's father transferred ownership of his company to two of his Christian colleagues, even though he continued to run the company through them. Anne and her older sister Margot were sent to an all-Jewish school.

ANNE FRANK (1941)

For Anne's thirteenth birthday in June of 1942, they gave her a journal with a red checkerboard cover. She pretended that she had a secret friend named "Kitty" and she wrote her first entry saying that she'd like to confide everything within the pages.

THE SECRET ANNEX

Then, in 1942, Anne's older sister Margot received a document that told her that she must go to a work camp located in Germany. The following day, the Frank family hid in what Anne later named their "The Secret Annex." The area where the Frank family remained in hiding was located in the rear part of the office building where her father worked.

Anne's parents as well as she and her sister lived in the small space for two years. Also living there was one of Otto's business partners, Hermann van Pels, with his wife and Peter, his son. In addition to the two families, there was a man by the name of Fritz Pfeffer.

ANNE FRANK HOUSE IN AMSTERDAM

1. THE WAREHOUSE
2. THE PRIVATE OFFICE AND KITCHEN
3. VICTOR KUGLER'S OFFICE
4. THE FRONT OFFICE OF MIEP GIES,
   JO KLEIMAN AND BEP VOSKUIJL
5. THE STOREROOM
6. THE LANDING WITH MOVABLE BOOKCASE

7. OTTO, EDITH AND MARGOT FRANKS ROOM
8. ANNE FRANK AND FRITZ PFEFFERS ROOM
9. THE BATHROOM
10. HERMAN AND AUGUSTE VAN PEL'S ROOM
11. PETER VAN PEL'S ROOM
12. THE ATTIC

everal people provided them with food as well as news about what was happening. They risked their own lives to do so.

The families and Pfeffer were stuck inside the dark, humid building for two years while they hid from the Nazis. While they were there, Anne wrote long entries in her diary every day. She wrote about the everyday feelings a teenage girl would have, but she also wrote about the suffering that millions of people in the world were experiencing.

er emotional stories were for her eyes only to begin with. It was a way for her to remain sane during the increasing horrors that were happening outside the Secret Annex.

DESTROYED COPY OF THE DIARY OF ANNE FRANK

Sometimes her writings were filled with despair, but just as often she retained a happy, optimistic outlook on life.

Snoezige foto hè !!!!

Ik zal
houver
nieman
ji Un
Ik heb
en vol aa
schrijf. a

Annelie

194

Ik ben

Her writing enabled her to cope with everything she and her family were going through. Her words and stories were filled with a wisdom and creativity that was unusual for a girl of her age.

CAPTURED BY THE NAZIS

After two years in hiding, an anonymous person told the Nazis where Anne and her family were. The Nazis broke into the Secret Annex and arrested the occupants. They were sent to Camp Westerbork, a transit camp in the northeastern region of the Netherlands. From there, they were shipped to a death camp in Poland known as Auschwitz.

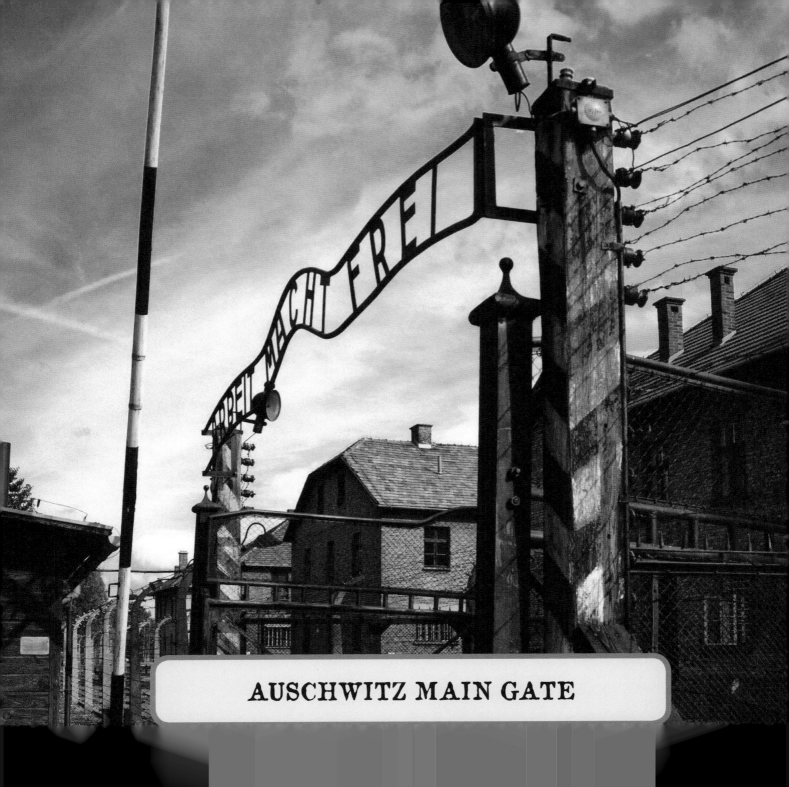

AUSCHWITZ MAIN GATE

They arrived on September 3rd of 1944 in the dead of night. Once in the concentration camp, the men and the women were separated. It was the last time Otto saw his family.

Anne and her sister were forced to carry heavy stones and mats of grass for months. They were transferred to the Bergen-Belsen camp located in Germany and their mother was not allowed to go with them.

Conditions at the Bergen-Belsen camp were unsanitary, food was very scarce, and the prisoners were contracting diseases in record numbers.

BERGEN-BELSEN CONCENTRATION CAMP

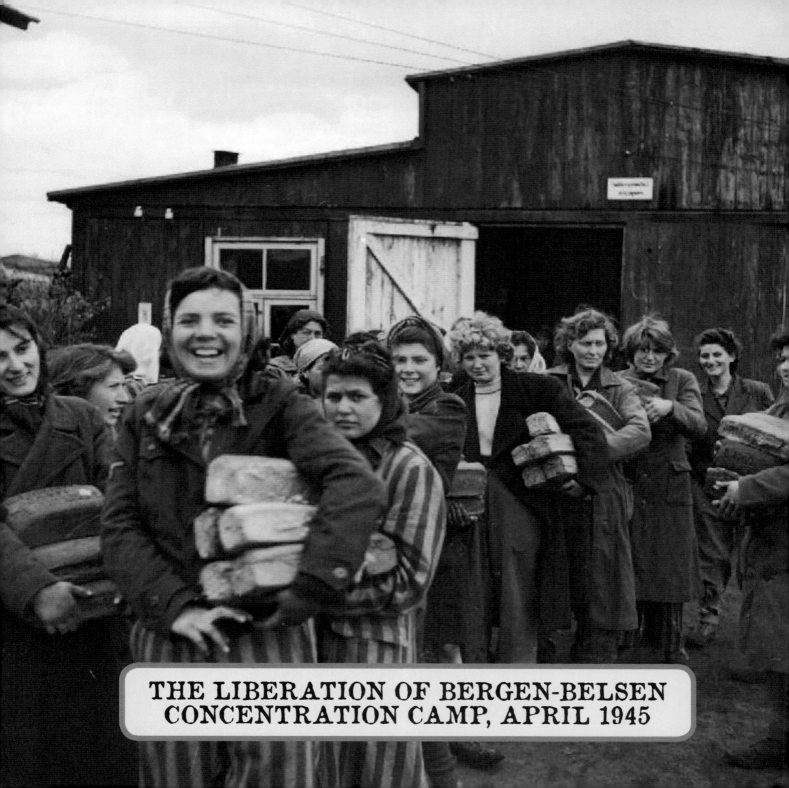

THE LIBERATION OF BERGEN-BELSEN
CONCENTRATION CAMP, APRIL 1945

Edith Frank died at Auschwitz in January of 1945. In March of that same year, Margot and Anne both contracted typhus and died. Anne was just 15 years of age when she died. More than 1 million children of the Jewish faith died during the Holocaust. A few weeks after Anne and her sister died, British soldiers set the prisoners at Bergen-Belsen free.

O tto Frank was the only person in Anne's family who survived the Nazi concentration camps. When the war was over, he went back to Amsterdam in the hopes that he could discover where his wife and daughters were

In July of 1945 he talked with two sisters who had been with his daughters at Bergen-Belsen. They told him what had happened to Margot and Anne. He mourned their deaths.

MIEP GIES AND OTTO FRANK (1961)

e also talked to Miep Gies. She had brought food to Otto and his family when they were in hiding. She had found Anne's journal and gave it to him.

When Otto finally felt mentally strong enough to read Anne's diary, he was amazed by Anne's wisdom and thoughts. It was a side of her that she had never shared with him. He found strength from reading what she had written and knew that others would too. He decided to publish it.

ANNE FRANK

HET
ACHTERHUIS

DAGBOEKBRIEVEN VAN
14 JUNI 1942 - 1 AUGUSTUS 1944

MET EEN INLEIDING VAN
ANNIE ROMEIN-VERSCHOOR

VIJFDE DRUK

AMSTERDAM
UITGEVERIJ CONTACT

**ORIGINAL COPY
OF THE BOOK**

Ejemplar de la Primera Edición del "Diario" publicado con el
nombre "La casa de atrás" en holandés, editado en 1949.
Perteneciente a Hedda Eisenstaedt, profesora de gimnasia de
Anne Frank en 1935 en Ámsterdam. Fue donado por sus hijos.

he Diary of Anne Frank was published on June the 25th in 1947. Eventually, Anne's diary was read by millions of people around the world. It has been translated to over 60 different languages.

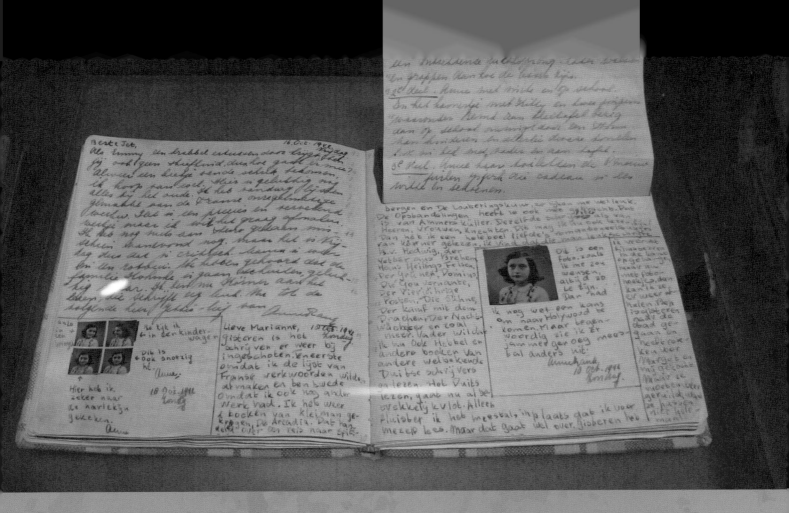

espite the passages that Anne wrote about her deep despair, her book holds a message of hope for the world. It stands as one of the most emotionally moving accounts of the experience of Jewish families during World War II.

THE ANNE FRANK HOUSE

After the war, the Secret Annex was scheduled for demolition but a group of people in Amsterdam fought to preserve it. Today, the Anne Frank House is one of the most popular museums in the city. You can see a three-dimensional version of the Secret Annex online.

HOUSE OF ANNE FRANK

SUMMARY

During World War II, Anne Frank, her parents, and her older sister were worried about what might happen to them after Hitler came into power in Germany. They were Jewish and as soon as Hitler became the leader of Germany, he began to institute policies that showed they were in danger.

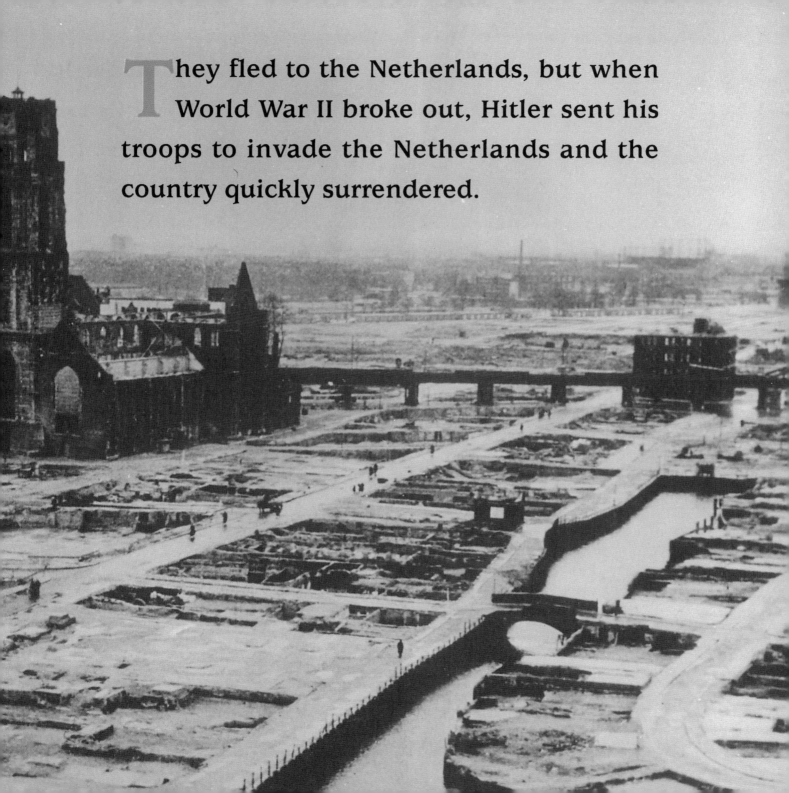

They fled to the Netherlands, but when World War II broke out, Hitler sent his troops to invade the Netherlands and the country quickly surrendered.

When Anne's sister, Margot was issued a notice saying that she would be taken to a camp, the Frank family hid in a Secret Annex behind the building where Anne's father worked.

ANNE FRANK'S STATUE

There, Anne, who was a budding writer, wrote extensive entries into a diary journal. They stayed in hiding for two years until the Nazis found them. Anne, her mother, and her sister died in the camps, but her father survived and eventually published Anne's work, which is now known around the world.

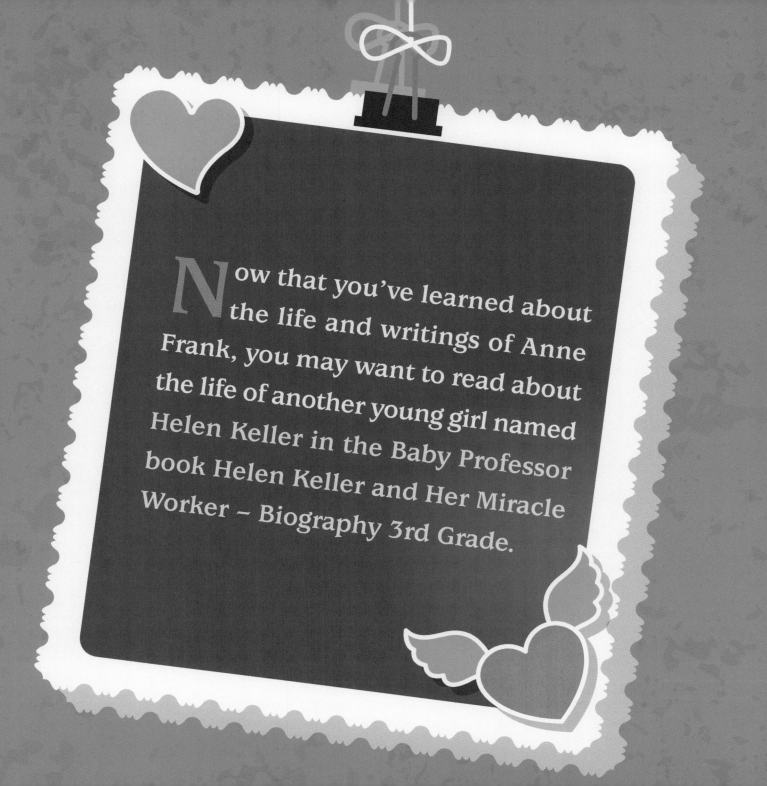

Now that you've learned about the life and writings of Anne Frank, you may want to read about the life of another young girl named Helen Keller in the Baby Professor book Helen Keller and Her Miracle Worker – Biography 3rd Grade.

Visit

BABY PROFESSOR
EDUCATION KIDS

www.BabyProfessorBooks.com

to download Free Baby Professor eBooks
and view our catalog of new and exciting
Children's Books

Printed in Great Britain
by Amazon

23215885R00039